Studies of the Exodus

Latrell Burns

Presentation by *BookLeaf Publishing*

Web: www.bookleafpub.com

E-mail: info@bookleafpub.com

ISBN: 9789360943561

First edition 2024

To Silas Mosby:

*Phenomenal Pastor and Spiritual leader for
many years*

A generous and kind-spirited gentleman

Hard working

*A loving Father, Grandfather,
Great-Grandfather,
Great-Great-Grandfather*

But above all else

He was and is God's Boy

Patience = Reward/Exodus
Part 1

Everyone on this earth has a small start
When God starts to work in your life, he makes
you a work of art
Far better than a Vincent van Gogh
All you have to do in return is let your light
show
Shine your light all around the world
God's love will become unfurled
You just have to do what He says
Don't say no, just say yes
If you say no you're denying your blessing
You are denying the same man who was
bleeding
Not just for you
But for the world you goof
Sorry for being briefly aloof
Your time will come, just be patient
And just for your benefit don't become
complacent
(circa July 29, 2015)

Exodus Part 2

When all seems lost for your family and friends
God is the one on whom you must depend
Use your talents and abilities to help them out
Even though you may think there is something
wrong with your mouth
Trust in the Lord, He'll bring you through
He'll even give you help out of the blue
So look to the Scriptures to guide your way
And God will make your crooked path straight
Relying on the Lord is the best thing you could
do
Trust me there are some things the Lord has
brought me through
Though this world may look like a man and soul
consuming zoo
Putting your Faith in God will make your soul
destruction-proof
So when your friends and family ask
you why do a certain thing
Simply say, "The Lord will give me a blessing"
(circa July 30, 2015)

Heavenly Man/Exodus Part 3

Just as the Lord delivered the Israelites
From the hands of the Egyptians
He allowed Yun (Brother Yun*) to shine his
Christian light
inside Chinese and Burmese prisons
Sure, there were times where both Israel and
Brother Yun doubted the Lord
Yet God delivered them both from the Devil's
sword
Put your reliance on the Lord for He will
provide for you
Despite your situation, He'll bring you through
He has healed Yun from multiple infirmities
And gave victory to the Israelite armies
Placing your faith and reliance in man
will end with you looking like the man who built
his house on sand
Or
If you're not careful enough
You'll be complacent too much and end up in
quicksand
So rely on the Lord and He'll bring you through
(circa Aug 3, 2015)
*For more context, look up Brother Yun or the
Heavenly Man*

Just the Beginning/Exodus
Part 4

Sometimes the Lord has to cut people out of
your life
That may have caused or was going to cause you
strife
So it is best to pray and meditate and watch the
Passover
Upon someone you may or may not hate
Just think of it as a fresh start or start over
For the Lord has something in store for you
And your biggest wish shall come true

Thank you Lord!

430 years is far too long to be enslaved
In order to stay out of captivity, behave
By doing and listening to what the Lord says
You will be saved in the physical world
But you must believe in Christ to be saved in the
Spiritual world

Chapter 12/Intermission

Jesus' blood he shed on the cross
Was the lamb's blood for the Passover
When it was correctly placed on the doorposts
The death angel couldn't kill the firstborn of
their houses
Jesus' blood covering us, is saving us from
eternal damnation
All those who don't have Jesus' blood upon them
will be sentenced to eternal damnation

The Journey Begins/Exodus
Part 5

The first-born in every family has a life of
responsibilities
From taking charge over your siblings
To when a parent is gone, make a living
Every firstborn should be consecrated and
blessed
Knowing that the Lord has destined them for
success
Though you may not be a firstborn
You should not look so forlorn
I would feel blessed to know that the firstborn is
watching out for me
And helping me when I get bullied
For it is only a matter of time
Before they get judgment for their crime
So thank you God for all the firstborns in the
world
Whether they're a boy or girl

A Praise Worthy God/ Exodus Part 6

Why do you grumble and complain so often
when you should be praising, worshiping and
blessing the Lord our God
Would you rather still be in Egypt
working in captivity until you were in your
coffin?
Or would you rather see what God has for you if
you just obey His Law
Be happy that you got out of Egypt without a
hitch
Because had it not been for God who delivered
you out, you'd be found in a ditch
So praise the Lord for what He has done
For the brief battle by the Red Sea He has won
The Escape was only the first step in God's plan
for you
Now that you are free, you know what to do
We must PRAISE Him!
For Deliverance
PRAISE Him!
For a New Beginning
PRAISE Him!
For His Mercy and Protection
Because without these things
You know where you would be

Ground Rules/Exodus Part 7

In order for us to have a new beginning
We must obey a set or several sets of ground
rules
10 of these laws, if obeyed, will give us a
blessing
All of the others are just for regulating

Listening to God and doing His will is key
Especially when time's crucial
Obeying the Lord has its benefits you'll see
He will bless you so much that you won't have
to live as if you're frugal

If only this nation could go back to laws that
were Bible-based
We could accomplish any challenge we faced
Believing and putting our faith and trust in the
Lord
Won't always land us in the prison ward

Mosaic Covenant/Exodus
Part 8

Thank you Lord for the Mosaic Covenant
By you, your people can multiply
Whatever land we want, you got it (if it's in His
Will)
All we have to do is believe and He will Provide
Yes, the Israelites got oxen blood on them
But we have Jesus' blood on us!
We simply have to think like the young lady
with the blood issue
"If I could just touch the hem of his garment, I
will be made whole"
As Christians today we need that type of Faith to
get what we need
Only in the Lord's will so we can proceed
Straight to the Promise Land with a different
leader
And possibly even with a different teacher
So keep your Faith and trust in the Lord and
whatever you ask for is yours

Instructions for Worship/ Exodus Part 9

God has brought you out of captivity
And granted you the Land of the Promised
Delivered you from slavery
So that Egypt you will not miss
He has granted you protection and blessings and
all you have to do is one thing
Build a Tabernacle according to His rules
And obey His laws to the Tee
If you read and obey His laws
He'll give you prosperity
If you're lucky,
beyond your physical measure
It will be a heavenly treasure
So stay on the path that God meant for you to be
God will enrich you spiritually

May God work through you day and night
Through happiness and sadness or 100% fright
May the Lord bless you continually
Prayer and supplication are the key

Don't Turn from Me, Follow the Path/Exodus Part 10

Don't turn from me
Follow the Path God sat out for you
Don't be crazy
Jesus Christ will be here soon
Attention all Americans and all those able
Turn to the book of Genesis and read about Cain
and Abel
Then give a grade to the state of the union
Because I would say we as a nation are unstable
Biblical principles are Abel and we are Cain
All this political or spiritual warfare is driving
me insane
It's time we made a new covenant with the Lord
In order to prevent a demon horde
To attack this nation
And send it to obliteration
I don't want America to be Sodom and
Gomorrah
And start using our heads like the ancient men in
togas
I may be telling the truth here,
Call me prolific
This is our year!
So Devil, you can stick it!

We are leaders and conquerors for the Lord
With God on our side to defeat a horde
Of demon filled militants from ISIS
Causing the Middle East to go into crisis
So God forgive us for our wrongdoings
And I thank you for showing me the light
Through my darkest night
While in fright
And giving me a spiritual sight
As to where this nation is going
I think I can hear the Lord's cavalry approaching

This was only the Beginning/ Exodus Part 11

This is only the beginning for God's people
The Construction of the Tabernacle well within
His Will
If we do what God says His Spirit will dwell
among us
And the power we are given through Him is
humongous
The power that is given to us comes from Jesus
So for any pastor, bishop, or clergy over a
church
There is a young Joshua waiting on their perch
Though you may have built that church from the
ground up
Don't give your ministry over to a weaker faith
chump
My apologies if that was too hard
I don't want to be hit by a destruction shard
When judgment day comes and the Evil One
begins his takeover
But all the saints will be singing "It ain't over."

The Finale/ Exodus Part 12

Yes, this is a finale to a God breathed series
Hopefully your eyes opened up so that you can
see clearly
All the principles and laws should be obeyed by
the nation
Except changed a little bit because of
modernization
We live in a country now where rules are bent
All of the things we see are not heaven sent
To all the leaders seeking instruction heed these
words
Stay on the path of Righteousness and rescue
these herds
So that they may glorify God
Even in places where it may seem kinda odd
And Lord be with Your Israelite people
Though they stray
They'll come back another day

God thank you for working through me on these
poems
I pray the Exodus reaches the people
I pray the Exodus poems and other manuscripts
reach fertile soil so that the Kingdom of God
may grow to new heights in this troubling time

Though Exodus may mean escape
I will go ahead and pull back the drape
To show you all who truly is Great
Especially without a debate

It is God, the Father, Head of the Trinity
To Him be all praise, honor, power, and the
glory
Creator of the world
And beyond superb at it
Far better at creating than you or I
This is the End of the Exodus
Thank you

Other Christian Faith based works

God's Near

Whenever you feel Alone
Or when you feel deserted
Just remember that God is there
When you're being bullied
Or you feel like you don't deserve it
Remember that God is near
Through every trial and tribulation
He'll bring you through
He is your rock and salvation
The Lion of Judah will take care of you
Crying in pain
Crying tears of joy
Jesus (He) heals the lame
Yes, Mary's baby boy
So if you're an outcast
Or you've been left alone
Like you're one of the last people on earth
without a home
Just put your problems in the hands of Jesus
And you won't break down into pieces

Easter Message

Your life is important
and so is mine
We will both leave soon
by and by
He has protected you and healed you all this
time
Every battle you fought, he was on your side.
Little known fact, he died for you too
This is something that most people won't do
Honestly, name someone you know who would
get:
Mocked, beaten, and cussed out for hours at a
time
He gave his life in exchange for you
In exchange for what could possibly be your end
destination
Accepting Him into your heart and you may be
welcomed to Heaven and the feast of
Unleavened Bread
Otherwise you may join the eternally dead
Jesus' blood shed for you and begged the
Heavenly Father too;
to let his poison cup pass from his lips and was
denied.
You can't even say a simple thank you?

Consider these thoughts when you're considering
sin
Jesus died for humanity once, He won't do it
again

Conquerors

Conquerors: Something that we're more than
This ability to be a conqueror was given to us
from God above
We are just like the Israelites searching for Land
As we search we are in His hands
The Land we search for is already ours
All thanks to God's Divine Powers
He's been helping us from day one
With help from his only Son
Guiding us along the way
We must always try to keep our paths straight
Every Christian is like an Israelite
Except we must keep our eyes on His light
Following this light will give us Victory
Following King Jesus is the Key
So no matter the trial or tribulation you're put
through
Just know that God will bring you through
God has made each of us conquerors
If you don't already see it now, stick around and
you'll see

Let Us See Him Together

Let us see Him together, my brothers and sisters
Christ is perfect and we are all sinners
Somewhere along the way we've been misled
All we are trying to do is keep our head off the
chopping block
And hopefully our heads above water
Because every parent will miss their son or
daughter
If they leave the path heading to Zion
They won't even have a shoulder to cry on
The misery and torture they will go through
Will be far worse in Hell if they don't stay true
Relying on the Almighty God will see them
through
'Cause the power He has in His hand atheists
have no clue
That He could end the world and start all over
anew if He felt necessary
Thus disproving every negative theory naysayers
have concocted

Therefore look up and let us see Him together
As brothers and sisters in Christ care for one
another
This world is far too dangerous and wild

for a young couple to raise a child
So we must be watchful of what Satan is doing
Because everyday millions of lives are being
enslaved
Just because they don't know the Lord
The Devil would rather have their bodies in the
dirt and their soils in his demonic horde
Ready to release at a moment's notice on anyone
When this time comes:

We must Look to the Hills from which our help
derives
He will be with us everyday of our lives as He
has been
Thankful to the One who died on Golgotha is an
excellent reason to be alive

So Difficult

Mark 10: 24 (NIV) "The disciples were amazed
at his words. But Jesus said again, "Children,
how hard it is to enter the kingdom of God!"

Funny way to start; call it odd
Jesus speaks the Truth
I am living proof
Of how difficult it is to secure a place in heaven
Getting this spot is more than taking part in the
Feast of unleavened
Prayer, supplication, and meditation are what I'm
prescribing as your medication
To let God use you anyway he chooses
If you let Satan do it, he will do nothing but
abuse you
Believe me when I write this and say
Being and staying on the Lord's side is the only
way;
For you to possibly reach Heaven
Because in this world today only 1 out of 7
people know who God is
And whom Christians send their praises to
Be cautious of what you do
Your seat in paradise may not be secure and
you'll have no clue

A Time for Everything (Ecc. 3:1- 8)

For Everything there is a season
God makes changes for a reason
and a time for every matter under heaven
Who knew life would be different after 9-11
A time to be born, and a time to die;
It's time to decide on whose side you lie
A time to plant, and a time to harvest
We're at a time in our lives where we have to try
our hardest
A time to kill, and a time heal;
Those in need would like a meal;
A time to breakdown,and a time to build up;
Enough goodbyes, I want to hear "what's up?"
A time to weep, and a time to laugh;
Let Jesus guide you with His rod and staff
A time to mourn, and a time to dance;
It's time to be a follower, not a fan
A time to clear away a whole field
Just to see what our seeds may yield
A time to embrace or maybe not
Because some people might still be hot
A time to seek, and a time to lose
Put your trust in God and just cruise
A time to keep, and a time to cast away

Some things in life just can't stay
A time to tear, and a time to mend
Most relationships work out because someone's
back must bend
A time to keep silent, and a time to speak boldly
Who knows, the words you say may be from the
Most Holy
A time to love, and a time to hate
This world we live in has gone irate
A time for war, and a time for peace
May God's blessings toward the reader of this
increase

Amen